DR. ANNEPAUL VEMAGIRI

From END to AND

First edition

This book was professionally typeset on Reedsy.
Find out more at reedsy.com

To all those who believe in the power of transformation and the journey from endings to new beginnings. This book is dedicated to the relentless seekers, the passionate learners, and the courageous change makers who turn every "end" into an "and." May your paths be filled with growth, discovery, and endless possibilities.

Contents

Preface

My book will inspire you if you are searching for yourself. After five decades of exploration, I've reached a profound conclusion.

You are your destination! You are your book, the answer to all your questions. Everything you seek is within you.

This book is my way of reconnecting with myself. Just like using Google Maps, we press the re-centre button when we lose our way. Life is similar; we often get disoriented, and that's natural. Find different ways to reach yourself. You are your vision, your own North Star. What you've been searching for is all within you.

Embrace your mistakes and accept them because falling and picking yourself up is part of the journey. You are the journey, and you are the destination. You are the author, and you are also the story. Whether you make it fictional or real, that choice is yours.

Five years ago, I embarked on the journey to write my book in my mind. I searched everywhere for inspiration and ideas, but in vain. The day I sat with myself AND my book happened. It was all inside me; I just had to sit with the person I am. What you read here is Annepaul Vemagiri writing Annepaul Vemagiri because you don't write a book; the book writes you.

Throughout this book, I narrate many instances in my life where I reached what felt like the END. But instead of stopping, I moved from "END" to "AND," creating an inspiring story of overcoming obstacles. These moments of transformation are the heart of my journey, showing that every END can be a new beginning; just learn to add an AND.

Let me walk you through my book and help you find yourself. Questions are a powerful way to provoke thoughts, so at the end of each chapter, I've left space for you to answer a powerful question to guide you on a journey within yourself. I hope you find out more about yourself through my book, just as I found out a little more about myself through writing my book.

Acknowledgments

Thank you, Mummy and Daddy, for bringing me into this world and creating a beautiful story through me. You truly brought forth a miracle. Today, you can be rest assured that your coming together is blessed.

Thank you, Usha, for being a parent and elder sister. When I wrote this book and visited my past places of life, I noticed you were majorly instrumental in my development.

Thank you, Vinay, Rachel, and Patrick, for being the best extended family in the world.

Thank you, Heena, for being the best coach in the world. You are the answer to my prayers.

CHAPTER 1

Journeys ...

THE JOURNEY OF MY NAME

My name's Journey from Anne to Dr. Annepaul Vemagiri has been quite an exploration. I am officially named after my aunt from Germany, whose name was spelt Anne without an "I." To my dear ones, I grew up being affectionately called "Choti" at home, which means little girl in Hindi.

Growing up as a person happened naturally; growing out of the name "Choti" required grit and determination. I struggled to rise above it and become someone who, despite being tiny, was powerful. In school, I was called Ann or Annie, often spelt incorrectly as the world was yet to learn to spell my name right. Moving into the working environment, I was called in more creative ways, which I ignored because I knew the world was still learning. Anne means "the gracious one," and I showed Grace when I was called incorrectly by having the patience to understand that the world takes time to take one full round.

Years later, when I was planning to move out of my homeland, I faced a hurdle with my passport renewal. When my new passport arrived, I noticed a fortunate flaw: my name was now connected to my father's, making it Annepaul Vemagiri. Paul, my dad's name, meant 'humble one.' This connected Humility to my Grace, making together one powerful woman I am today.

With time, I realized this change brought clarity and opened doors to breakthroughs, including travelling to foreign lands and achieving higher positions of power.

I decided to keep the name Annepaul Vemagiri as it was officially declared. This name has become a significant part of my identity and journey. Before I reached my half-century life milestone, I stamped my name with the title Doctor. AND today, I am addressed as Dr. Annepaul Vemagiri.

Life is a
journey, not
a destination

Reflecting on this journey, I feel a deep sense of gratitude and pride. Moving forward, I aspire to continue embracing new challenges and opportunities with the same resilience and determination that have brought me this far. I can fondly recount all those conversations where my name became significant today.

Mother: "Choti, come here! It's time for dinner. "Me: "Coming, Mom!" Teacher: "Ann, please come to the board and solve this problem?" Me: "It's Anne. But sure, I'll give it a try."

Colleague: "Hey, Annie! Can you help me with this report?"

Me: "It's Anne Paul, but yes, I can help."

Passport Officer: "Your new passport is ready. Here you go, Annepaul Vemagiri."

Me: "Wait, what? Annepaul Vemagiri? Well, I guess that's my new name now."

Manager: "Dr. Annepaul Vemagiri, congratulations on your doctorate!"

Me: "Thank you! It feels surreal to achieve this milestone finally."

The journey of my name is fascinating.

Each END to a name began a new phase of 'AND,' where a new name called me. It started with what others wanted me to be called and evolved into what I wanted others to call me. These moments of transformation are the heart of my journey, showing that every end can be a new beginning.

Each name felt like a station in the train called life, where Dr. Annepaul Vemagiri seemed to be the last station. Oh, yes! One name is remaining—the name the world will remember me by when I move into my heavenly ride.

What has been your inspiration to read this book ?

THE JOURNEY OF MY SIGNATURE

On a usual day at home, when everyone else planned to rest and relax, I was found with my head dipped into a spread of old notebooks. My tiny fingers were struggling to grip and write something with ease. I was age 7, and my old notebooks had few pages left. I made a pile of those notebooks, imitating my teachers at school. I wrote a new name on each notebook and wrote the same questions in all notebooks, but I changed the answers randomly. My tiny fingers would work like a grown-up teacher. I knew the questions, the answers, and the scores.

At the end of this exercise, I took the pen my father had given me and started to correct all the notebooks. Once I corrected and gave scores, I would then sign underneath. I would put my name and then also give a designation—General Manager. My mind fails to understand where I picked up those words.

That moment, while I was busy correcting my notebooks, my sister walked in and asked, "Choti, what are you doing?"

I looked up with a smile and said, "I'm being the General Manager!"

She laughed and replied, “Do you even know what a General Manager does?”

I shook my head and said, “No, but it sounds powerful, doesn’t it?”

She nodded thoughtfully and said, “Well, whatever it is, I’m sure you’ll be great at it. You always put your heart into everything you do.” Her words stayed with me, reinforcing my belief in the power of dreams and determination.

As I reflect on my journey, I’m reminded of an inspiring quote by Eleanor Roosevelt:

“The future belongs to those who believe in the beauty of their dreams.”

My journey moved upward like my signature, representing growth and progress. My dreams were the roots, and my sister’s words became the fertilizer. So, instead of taking the lane of ‘the END’ at the junctures of failures in life, I chose another ‘AND’ and continued to add more ‘ANDs’ to my dreams.

It’s incredible how a simple act like signing my name as “General Manager” as a little kid sparked a lifelong journey towards empowerment and owning my life story. This passion for learning and the sense of authority I felt while correcting notebooks is a beautiful memory. I love to visit to find inspiration when my cup is empty and I am looking for a refill.

It's fascinating how childhood dreams and actions can shape our future paths. My story shows that the seeds of ambition and purpose can be planted early on, even if we don't fully understand them then.

What was your aspiration as a child ?

THE JOURNEY OF MY CAREER

My journey from a teacher to a lecturer, from a lecturer to an Assistant Professor and then from a Manager to a Corporate Head of Learning & Development has been another roller coaster ride.

Returning to my story of correcting notebooks and putting those ticks, today, when I connect back the dots, I realize that it was a glimpse of a little trainer in me who used to relish accessing the power through correcting copies. I knew it back then, even if I didn't fully understand it. If you ask me what one word made me who I am today, my answer would be "tick." Yes, the symbol of a tick, which signifies "all OK."

I was fascinated by the corrections my teachers made in our notebooks. When no correction was needed, the tick was the signature authority to signify that "all is well." How just an arched line could authenticate the world of words on paper!

I wasn't someone who enjoyed pointing out mistakes. I enjoyed the authority and power the tick brought.

Post-graduation, I drifted to working in a hotel, which I left with an instinct to take up a teaching job where my heart felt at peace. From being a teacher to a lecturer and then an Assistant Professor were the stepping stones that I walked with ease, even though each time the stone I stepped on was bigger than the previous one.

My career cycle moved from stepping on stones to climbing the ladders from Training Manager to Human Resources Manager and then from Director of Training to Cluster Director of Training, and now I am heading the entire training department of my growing organization.

Over the years, I climbed the steps individually, embracing each challenge and opportunity. I moved from putting ticks on notebooks to ticking all the career boxes I had set for myself. Each tick represented a milestone achieved, a goal met, and a new level of growth.

With each milestone, I didn't see it as an 'END' but as an "AND"—an opportunity to start a new chapter in my career. This mindset allowed me to view every achievement not as a destination but as a step up to something greater. Each accomplishment allowed me to build on my experiences, learn new skills, and take on new challenges.

"What Got You Here Won't Get You There"

This famous book title was my mantra. I always worked as if I were already in a higher position. I behaved so real that moving up felt natural with time. Embodying the qualities and behaviours of the position I aspire to has been incredibly powerful. This called for being proactive and intentional.

When I transitioned from a teacher to a Lecturer, I didn't see it as the end of my teaching journey. Instead, it was an "AND"—an opportunity to delve deeper into academia, influence more students, and refine my teaching methods. Moving from a lecturer to an Assistant Professor was not just a promotion; it was an "AND"—a chance to engage in research, mentor junior faculty, and contribute to the academic community in more meaningful ways.

When I became a Training Manager, it wasn't the culmination of my career in training. It was an "AND"—an opportunity to explore the corporate world, understand the dynamics of adult learning, and develop comprehensive training programmes. Each subsequent role, from Human Resources Manager to Director of Training and then to Cluster Director of Training, represented another 'AND'—a new chapter filled with growth, innovation, and leadership possibilities.

This perspective helped me remain open to continuous learning and adaptation. It encouraged me to embrace change and seek new opportunities, knowing each milestone was just the beginning of another exciting journey. By viewing my career through the lens of 'AND' rather than 'END,' I maintained a forward-looking attitude, always ready to take on the next challenge and achieve new heights.

Where in your career did you feel like it was 'The END', but it turned out to be an 'AND'?

THE JOURNEY FROM GUAVA TO GRAVITY

Coming back from school was always an exciting part of my day. I would run straight to the orchard where my favorite guava tree stood.

Every day, I knew precisely how many guavas were ripe and how many were still green. The crunch of that fresh bite and the tangy flavor rejuvenated me, and the color of the guavas excited me. That time spent with the guava tree was my special "me time" as a child, and I never wanted to share it with anyone else.

"Look at these beauties," I would whisper, gently touching the ripe guavas. "Tomorrow, you'll be ready."

There was also the jungle jalebi, or Pithecellobium dulce, commonly known as Manila tamarind, Madras thorn, monkeypod tree, or camachile. I would carry a long stick to pluck the fruits, which felt like the reward for my evening labour.

"Gotcha!" I would exclaim triumphantly as I knocked down an exceptionally high fruit. "You're mine now."

Childhood was all about spending time with myself and my favourite fruits. I never wanted to play with other kids, possibly because I couldn't match their energy or compete with them. It was during those moments that I realised I was different.

"Why don't you come to play with us?" a friend would ask. "I like it here," I would reply, smiling and holding up my freshly picked fruits. "This is my happy place."

Later, when I was diagnosed with arthritis, it confirmed that I was indeed different. This diagnosis explained why I preferred my own company and why I couldn't keep up with the other children. Despite the challenges, those solitary moments in the orchard brought me immense joy and peace. They were a significant part of my childhood, shaping who I am today.

"You're special," my parents would say, comforting me. "And that's perfectly okay."

As I grew older, I learnt to embrace my uniqueness and the faith that had always guided me. Martin Luther King, Jr.'s words resonated deeply: "Faith is taking the first step even when you don't see the whole staircase." Every day, I took small steps toward understanding and accepting myself, even when the future seemed uncertain.

In the quiet moments under the guava tree, I found solace in Rabindranath Tagore's wisdom:

"Faith is the bird that feels the light when the dawn is still dark."

Tagore's words, indeed, touch my soul and guide me through uncertain times.

Finding my gravity under the guava tree was a transformative experience, much like Newton's discovery under the apple tree. In those quiet moments, I felt a profound connection to the world around me. The guava tree became a symbol of my journey towards self-discovery and understanding.

Just as Newton's apple tree led him to the laws of gravity, my guava tree helped me realize the importance of faith and introspection. It was under its branches that I found clarity and direction, guiding me through life's uncertainties. This serene spot became my sanctuary, where I could reflect, dream, and find the strength to move forward.

Looking back, those moments in the orchard were more than just childhood memories; they were lessons in faith and resilience. They taught me to believe in myself and to find joy in the simple, solitary moments.

Moving from 'END' to my childhood, I grew with an 'AND' to a journey within me.

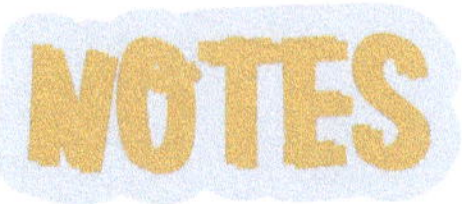

What has been your gravity Tree or place as a child?

THE JOURNEY FROM SKIN TO SHINE WITHIN

I grew up with dark skin, and for three decades, I felt ashamed and incredibly shy, believing I lacked something significant. These impressions were shaped by the comments and jokes people made about me when I was young. Words like "black fruit," "black pencil," and "so dark" cut deeper than my skin. I lived hating my colour, convinced that no guy would ever fall in love with me because of my complexion.

"Who would marry her?" I heard him say, and I believed those words possibly until today. This constant ridicule built an inferiority complex within me. The jokes about my colour eroded my confidence as a young woman. AND to fill that void, I began focusing on my intellect.

One day, I overheard a conversation between two classmates.

"Did you see her? She's so dark," one whispered.

"Yeah, I wouldn't want to be friends with her," the other replied.

These words stung, and I felt a wave of sadness wash over me.

I often felt that people secretly made comments about me. I believed that others didn't want to be friends with me because of my dark colour. I even felt that children wouldn't want to come close to me because of my skin complexion. These feelings of isolation and rejection were incredibly painful.

To cope, I immersed myself in books, learning, and developing my skills. One evening, my mother noticed my dedication.

"You've been studying a lot lately," she said, her voice filled with concern.

"I just want to be good at something," I replied, trying to hide the hurt in my voice. I remember my mother would always say, "She is dark, but she is beautiful." My mother spoke about me with pride in her eyes, and that kept me going toward exploring my inner beauty.

She would daily scrub my delicate skin using gram flour and curd with turmeric. She would massage my skin to shine with her pure hands.

"Your skin is beautiful," she would say as she gently massaged the mixture onto my skin.

"One day, you'll see it too." She would remind me, "Beauty is not about the skin colour, but your substance, which you bring to the world. Your values will make you beautiful, and you are already beautiful."

I discovered a passion for knowledge and a talent for problem-solving. Over time, I realized that my worth was not tied to my appearance but to my abilities and character. I started to see the beauty in my skin and the strength in my journey.

My shift from skin to shine within happened when I started learning to coach. During many sessions, I focused on diving deeper beyond my skin to find answers to heal me. These sessions, which initially started as practice, showed signs of healing as I noticed the difference in my perspectives. I realized that beauty is colourful and not just one colour. My mind had the power to make others notice in me what I wanted them to. People see in us what we focus on in ourselves. It's that simple. That's when I started focusing on my personality, making it so big that everything else would hide behind its size.

"Beauty begins the moment you decide to be yourself." by Coco Chanel

This quote underlines the idea that true beauty comes from authenticity. When you embrace who you truly are, without trying to conform to others' expectations, you radiate a unique and genuine beauty.

Through this process, I found activities that helped me build confidence and self-acceptance. I met people who appreciated me for who I was, not for how I looked. Their support and kindness helped me heal and grow. I learnt to love myself and embrace my uniqueness.

One day, a friend said to me, "You know, your skin is beautiful. It's a part of who you are, and it makes you unique."

Her words touched my heart, and I smiled, feeling a warmth I hadn't felt in years.

Today, I get compliments for my skin tone, and now we know who chiselled me using gram flour and curd with turmeric to make me look like the diamond I am.

Now, I stand tall, proud of my dark skin and the person I've become. My mindset has shifted from "I am ashamed of my skin colour" to "I am beautiful," and this transformation has been a journey of self-discovery, acceptance, and empowerment.

An 'END' to a mind where the words of others influenced my personality to a new mindset where I began to think starting with an 'AND' I know I am beautiful.

What were you ashamed of yourself as a child?

THE JOURNEY OF MY MOM'S FAVORITE SINGER

I was the nightingale of my family, singing at every corner of our house. My mom always said, "You have the voice of an angel."

My dad worked on the railways, so we used to go to the railway club where events were conducted, and children were invited to perform.

During Independence Day celebrations, I recited a patriotic song. At the end of the song, everyone stood up to clap. "Wow, what a feeling that was!" I thought to myself, beaming with pride. Both my parents admired me for this talent.

My mother would often ask, "Can you sing that song I love?" And I would happily oblige, singing different numbers for her. Growing up, I performed many times on stage. I was also a choir singer in my church.

When my mom left this world, I was devastated. "How can she be gone?" I whispered to myself, tears streaming down my face. I lived in the shock of realizing that mothers are mortal beings. It took me a long time to gather myself and celebrate life through singing again. When I tried to restart my life, I found that I had lost not only my mother but also my voice. I couldn't sing. I choked and sweated whenever I was asked to sing.

Ten years passed by until my sister encouraged me to sing again. "You have to sing for Mom," she said gently. She advised me to take singing classes, so I enrolled. At first, I felt my voice was empty. "I can't do this," I muttered during practice. I couldn't sing even a line. But at the insistence of my sister, I practiced. She further suggested, "Why don't you enroll in a renowned singing certification program?" I did that, and by the end of the program, I passed with distinction at level 103 in classical singing.

My inspiration to start again was to bring my mother back into my life through her favourite songs. Singing helped me to heal from the inside. "I did it," I whispered to myself, feeling a sense of accomplishment. I still struggle, but I am not giving up because I am my mother's favourite singer.

What is that one childhood Talent you lost, and how do you plan to bring it back?

THE JOURNEY OF MOVING A MOUNTAIN

I read, and I heard, "If you have faith as small as a mustard seed, you can say to this mountain, 'Move from here to there,' and it will move. Nothing will be impossible for you." And this was the game changer. Those words in black written on white sheets left no grey area to doubt. They were loud and clear as the words made eye contact with me and were determined to make a lifetime impact on me.

Words, I think, are angels who walk into our lives in shapes we can comprehend. When these words are positive, they become powerful tools to shape our lives. Some of these words, especially the word faith, stood out from the rest.

I started pondering its meaning, and to me, it meant trust. I walked to my tiny shelf of books to find the rusted dictionary. I hurried to find the page where the word "trust" was found, and it read, "Faith is confidence or trust in a person, thing, or concept.".

I thirst more for a deeper meaning, and then I closed my eyes to look within me. That's when I got my answer: Faith means action. Would we act if we don't have faith/hope? Growing up was a blend of joy and struggles. My childhood was painted with moments of innocence, a yearning for adventure, and, eventually, a shadow of pain. I distinctly remember the afternoons when school was over.

I recollected that as soon as I walked down from the school, I would throw my bag at the corner of the house, kick off my shoes, and dart away to that guava tree hidden behind the farthest end of our garden, my secret haven. The branches welcomed me like an old friend, and I would sit there for hours, pretending I was the queen of a magical land where no one could reach me. "Daddy," I would often ask, my voice full of curiosity, "when will I learn to fly?"

My father would chuckle, "Many moons from now, but until then, enjoy the fruit of your childhood tree."

But freedom felt limited for me. I wasn't a healthy child. My pale skin often made people comment, "She looks weak.". My legs would ache after walking too far, and sometimes, even short distances felt like an uphill climb.

One day, when I was twelve, I told my father, "Daddy, my bones feel like they're cracking." He stopped mid-sentence, the newspaper in his hand trembling slightly. "Cracking? Show me where."

I couldn't point to one place. It was everywhere. That's when the doctor's visits began.

"Rheumatoid arthritis," the doctor said after running tests. His voice was calm and clinical, but it sounded like thunder in my ears.

"What does that mean?" I asked, looking between my parents. My mother's lips quivered before she forced a smile. "It's nothing, Choti. Just some pain. You'll be fine with the medicine." The medicine came in colourful pills and bitter syrups. Worse, there were calcium injections. Each prick felt like a betrayal. "I hate this!" I shouted one evening, tears streaming down my cheeks.

My mother knelt beside me. "I know, Choti. But these prayers," she held my hands tightly, "these prayers will make everything better."

Her faith became my anchor. Despite the pain, she would insist I accompany her to church every Sunday. One Sunday, during a children's class, the teacher read out the verse,

"If you have faith as small as a mustard seed, you can move mountains."

That night, I lay in bed, staring at the cracks in the ceiling. "Daddy," I whispered when he came to check on me.

"Hmm?"

"What if my pain is my mountain? Do you think I can move it?"

He sat down beside me, brushing a strand of hair from my forehead. "Mountains don't move on their own. You need faith, yes, but you also need action. Do you think you're ready for that?"

I didn't answer then, but something shifted inside me. The next morning, I woke up determined. For me, faith wasn't just belief; it was action. So, in my naivety, I began throwing away the pills. Whenever my mother wasn't looking, I would empty them into the trash or flush them down the toilet. "Aren't you feeling better?" my father asked one evening when I managed to walk around the garden without wincing.

I smiled faintly. "I think the prayers are working."

But deep down, I was terrified. What if the pain returned? What if my act of rebellion brought consequences I couldn't bear? My mountain loomed larger than ever.

As I transitioned from my teenage years to adulthood, I clung to three pillars: action, my mother's unwavering prayers, and the ability to move on. Each time fear crept in, I whispered to myself, "Faith like a mustard seed." When I turned twenty-one, I completed my Hotel Management degree and landed a job in Hyderabad. It was my first step away from home, away from the protective cocoon of my parents. I threw myself into work, forgetting the shadow of pain that had followed me for years. One day, as I was organizing a guest's itinerary, it hit me: I hadn't felt pain in months.

I called my father that evening. "Daddy," I began hesitantly, "Do you remember what the doctor said about the wheelchair?" "Of course," he replied, his voice heavy with memory. He hesitated to mention that the doctor had said that when I would be 25 years of age, I would be in a wheelchair. "I... I think he was wrong." I have won victory over the mountain and I am on the mountain-top.

There was a pause before he chuckled softly. "Sometimes, Choti, even doctors underestimate the power of faith."

Years passed, and the memory of those injections, those sleepless nights, faded. But the lessons remained. Now, at fifty, I look back and marvel at the experience. The doctor's grim prediction had failed. I wasn't bound to a wheelchair. Instead, I stood tall, a testament to faith, prayer, and resilience.

One usual morning, the room was bathed in the soft glow of morning light streaming through the floor-to-ceiling windows. The walls were adorned with awards and motivational quotes, each one a testament to the hard work and perseverance that had defined her journey. Sitting there on a queen-like office chair and ready to take over the world was me. A framed photograph of my late parents placed strategically on my desk caught my eye as I paused to sip my drink—pure water. It had been exactly 6 months since my dad passed away, and I had lost Mom 18 years back.

My thoughts were interrupted by a soft hello at the door. "Hey! "I said, my voice firm yet warm. He paused momentarily, noticing my lightly moist eyes and the photo I had been gazing at.

"Anne," he began hesitantly, "the moisture in your eyes seems to speak volumes about the love and respect you have for your parents. I've often wondered, what keeps you moving mountains with zeal and energy? I'm sure your parents have a role in these stories."

I leaned back in my chair, a faint smile playing on my lips. "You're right, Aakash. My parents were my greatest teachers, my unwavering pillar of strength. Everything I am today is because of the lessons they imparted. As I was speaking, my mind drifted back to moments of my childhood, vivid memories that were etched into my soul. Each one was a chapter of love, guidance, and growth.

In moments when I stumbled, and laughter filled the air,
Their smile was always a beacon of their care.
They guided me through shadows, with wisdom in their eyes,
Showing me the way, beneath the endless skies.
They laid the path before me, unseen but always true,
Silent guardians, in everything I'd do and still do
With gentle hands, they lead me to the brink,
Encouraging each leap, when I was scared to think.
Through valleys deep and wide, they lift me in their arms,
A fortress of protection, shielding me from harms.
In every step and stride, their love was always near,
Parents endless strength, forever holding dear.

What has been your mountain in life you would like to move?

THE JOURNEY OF MY CAREER GRAPH

That night, my sister Usha's words echoed in my mind, refusing to let me rest. "So, what are you doing about it? Do not sleep until you have done something about it," she had said, her tone sharp yet full of care. Those words felt like a spark in a dark room, igniting a fire deep within me.

I sat on the edge of my bed, the quiet hum of the ceiling fan above doing little to soothe the storm inside me. My mind raced, my chest tight with both determination and fear. The night stretched endlessly, but I knew one thing: I wouldn't sleep until I took action. It was 2011, and I was in Bangalore, working at a hotel management college. I had only been there for two months, yet the weight of the past year felt like it might crush me.

I thought back to my father's words, spoken many years ago, that had carried me through some of the darkest times of my life: "Take care of yourself and don't worry about earning money. Money will come. Just focus on your journey." His voice, warm and steady, played in my mind like a melody from my childhood.

Life moves forward in the direction of the choices we make

My father had been my anchor since the day I lost my mother. He had become our mother and father, filling every role with love, wisdom, and an almost magical positivity.

But even his wisdom couldn't have prepared me for 2010. That year, I got married, full of hope and dreams for the future. I still remember the excitement in my father's eyes as he walked me down the aisle, his hand steady on mine. But within a month, it all fell apart. The marriage crumbled, leaving me devastated, alone, and questioning my worth. The grief was a weight I carried every day, pressing down on my chest and stealing my breath. Nights were the hardest. I would sit in the dark, staring at the ceiling, tears streaming silently as I tried to understand how my life had crumbled so quickly.

Life took a dip, and in 2011, I found myself in Bangalore, working for a renowned hotel school, but I felt disconnected and knew I didn't belong there. Now my new stepping stone had to be on newer ground.

How can I forget that power-packed conversation I had with my sister that night when she was my final rescue after I tried all possible ways to recuperate?

I called my sister, "I can't sleep. I'm feeling so anxious about everything," I said.

"I get it. What's on your mind?" She asked without worry and with a certainty that she was in control of the conversation.

"I just feel stuck. I don't know what to do next." I said with a low voice. "It's okay to feel that way. Sometimes, things just need time to fall into place. Have you thought about what you want to do?" she tried to probe. "I guess I just want some direction. Maybe a new job or something."

"If you want a new job, then find one. Do not sleep tonight until you have applied to all possible vacancies", she said firmly and clearly. "Yeah, you're right. I'll start looking right now." I got excited. She continued, "When you want something, then do something about it"

She made the point clear and disconnected.

I opened my laptop and switched on the Wi-Fi. It was late in the night, around 11 pm. I opened sites for jobs and started applying to all possible places I thought I fit in. My sister's words kept my eyes wide open to opportunities, and I dived in through a tick on the apply button. I did this until I knew I had done enough.

I woke up without expectations as my efforts were my achievements that morning, and until around 11 am, I received a call for an interview.

"Good morning! Is this Anne Paul?" the voice on the other end asked. "Yes, speaking," I replied, my heart racing. "We'd like to invite you for an interview for the position of Training Manager," they said. What happened next was the tip of the iceberg.

I got an opportunity to work for one of the biggest hospitality brands, where I spent nearly five of my best years in Chennai. I was offered the position of Training Manager. The organization was looking for a candidate from academics, and I was the one. That was the first time I truly listened with intent to the word "training" and began my journey of learning and unlearning all aspects of this newfound love.

That single opportunity became the first in a series of events that would transform my life. Each interview, each job offer, felt like a piece of a puzzle falling into place. From being a pre-opening Training Manager to becoming the Head of Learning and Development in the Maldives, every step of my journey was an attestation to resilience and the power of action.

"Daddy," I called him one evening after receiving my first major promotion. My voice wavered as I said, "I'm scared. What's next?

His laughter on the other end of the line was like a balm to my soul. "Choti," he said, his voice steady and reassuring, "You've already climbed the mountain. This is just the view. Enjoy it."

His words stayed with me, a reminder to embrace every moment, no matter how daunting. But it was Usha who kept pushing me forward. She called me regularly, her voice brimming with excitement and determination. "What's next? What are you aiming for now?" she'd ask, never letting me settle or grow complacent.

At 38, when most people were looking to slow down, I was just getting started. I had spent years building myself back up, piece by piece, and now, I was ready to soar. Sitting in my office in the Maldives, I looked at the awards lining my desk—three awards, a doctorate, and countless moments of recognition. Each one felt like a victory, not just over external challenges but also over the doubts and fears that had once held me captive.

One evening, as the sun dipped below the horizon, painting the sky in hues of orange and pink, Usha called. "Do you ever stop to think about how far you've come?" she asked, her voice soft but insistent.

I looked out of the window, the ocean stretching endlessly before me. "Sometimes," I admitted. "But it's not just mine; it's ours—your words, Daddy's wisdom—they're the reason I'm here."

That strength became my mantra. Every setback became a lesson, and every challenge an opportunity. When people asked me how I managed to rebuild my life, I would smile and say, "Doing something about it."

But it was more than that. It was about the people who believed in me and who refused to let me give up. It was about the nights I cried, only to wake up stronger. It was about those small steps that led to giant leaps.

AND today, as I stand at the crossroads of new opportunities, I carry those words with me. Usha's encouragement, my father's wisdom, and my resilience have brought me here. And while the journey is far from over, I know one thing for certain: I will keep moving forward, taking action, and never letting adversity define me. The fire ignited that night still burns brightly, lighting my path.

Reflecting on my journey, I realize that moving from my 'END' to 'AND' was a transformative process. It wasn't just about overcoming a single obstacle but about embracing a mindset of continuous growth. Each challenge I faced became an opportunity to learn and evolve. The support of my loved ones, especially Usha's unwavering encouragement and my father's pearls of wisdom, played a crucial role in this transformation.

I learnt that every setback is not an END but a chance to pivot AND find new paths. By taking action, no matter how small, I was able to rebuild my life piece by piece. This journey taught me the power of perseverance and the importance of believing in oneself.

AND today, as I stand at the threshold of new opportunities, I carry with me the lessons of the past and the strength to face the future. My story is a burning proof of the fact that with determination and support, we can turn our 'END' into 'AND,' opening doors to endless possibilities.

The only limit to our realization of tomorrow is our doubts of today." — Franklin D. Roosevelt

This quote beautifully reflects how overcoming self-doubt and taking action can transform our lives.

THE JOURNEY FROM AVERAGE TO DISTINCTION

My marks in my 12th grade were average, precisely 48%. But these numbers didn't stop me from pursuing my education. I had a hunger to study, which came from the energy that was missing in my body due to my physical sickness. I used this energy to fuel my academic journey.

I completed my bachelor's degree in Hotel Management, followed by a Master's in Business Administration and a Master's in Tourism Management. In 2024, I achieved my Doctorate in Learning & Development. Along the way, I also completed several other certifications and courses listing a few AND,

Time to pat my back for the list here

- Master Trainer Certification from Rotana Hotels, Abu Dhabi,
- Master Trainer Program—Teaching, Training & Developing Professionals endorsed by NCC Education
- Master NLP Practitioner Course by Anil Dagia, Pune, India
- Certificate in Power BI with distinction from ExcelR

- Distinguished Learning & Development Professional from AON
- Post-Graduation Diploma in Human Resources from IGNOU, India,
- Financial Mindset, Emotional Mastery Coach, and Employee Relationship Coach training from Anil Dagia
- Diploma in Storytelling Course from Kathalaya, Bangalore, India
- Digital Marketing Course from www.socialprachar.com, Hyderabad, India
- Write Way Certification on Writing Skills from Writernaama
- Business English Train the Trainer from British council
- Train The Trainer from Dale Carnegie
- Train The Trainer from various Hospitality Brands: Rotana, Millennium, and Hyatt Hotels
- Hyatt on Skills from Hyatt, Chennai, India
- Certification for handling guests with special needs from Qatar Tourism Authority, Doha
- Google Certified Trainer (Online) from Google
- Lakme Make-up Course from Lakme Academy, Hyderabad, India
- Courses on Learning Foreign Languages—French, German, Spanish, and Japanese
- Talent Optimization Leadership Course from PI
- Training from Rotana: Master Trainer, Group Training Skills, Coaching, Mentoring, Interviewing & Selection Skills, Performance Management, Destination Leadership.

"Success is not final, failure is not fatal: It is the courage to continue that counts." - Winston Churchill

This quote by Winston Churchill emphasizes the importance of continuing. It reminds us that achieving success is not the end of the journey. Success is a milestone, but it doesn't mean we can stop striving for improvement or new goals. Similarly, failure is not the end of the road. It is a temporary setback that provides valuable lessons and opportunities for growth.

The true measure of a person's character and determination lies in their ability to keep moving forward, regardless of the obstacles they face. Courage is the key to overcoming challenges and continuing the pursuit of one's dreams and aspirations. It is the courage to persist, to learn from failures, and to keep pushing toward success that ultimately defines our journey. My story is a perfect example of this quote in action. Despite the initial low scores, I demonstrated courage and determination to achieve distinctions and numerous qualifications.

List all that your learnings here

CHAPTER 2

Circle of Life ...

LIFE IS A FULL CIRCLE

The night after my mother passed away, my father gathered us around the dinner table. His voice was steady, yet gentle, as he spoke words that would shape our grief into something more profound. "Why are you sad? Why are you crying?" he asked, looking at each of us in turn. "Your mother has not gone far. She's just moved closer to God. She's sitting right next to Him now. Whatever you need, just ask her. She will ask God for you, and your wishes will be granted."

Those words, spoken with such conviction, brought a fragile smile to my face and my elder sister's face. My younger brother, usually stoic, nodded quietly, his eyes glistening with unshed tears. That night, my father's faith became our anchor.

It was 2007 when we lost our mother to lung cancer. She was a beautiful soul, radiant in her kindness and love. She was passionate about cooking and took joy in feeding everyone who came to our home. "Food is love," she would say, handing me a plate of freshly made parathas. Her laughter filled every corner of our house, a melody that seemed eternal. But life had other plans.

I was living in Bangalore when my father's call came. "Choti, your mother is unwell. She's in the ICU," he said, his voice calm but heavy with the weight of the truth he didn't speak. I rushed home, convinced she would recover. "She's strong," I told myself. But 24 days later, we lost her.

In the months that followed, my father became both parents to us. He filled the void with his unwavering positivity and strength. He turned every challenge into an opportunity for joy.

When bills piled up, he'd say, "At least we have each other." When I felt overwhelmed with work, he'd remind me, "Your mother's watching. Make her proud." One evening, as I struggled to balance my job and my emotions, he sat beside me. "Choti, do you know what your mother loved most about you?"

I shook my head. "What?"

"Your determination. She always said you had a fire in you, a spark that could light up the darkest rooms. Don't let that fire go out."

His words stayed with me, carrying me through the toughest days. In 2024, when my father passed away, I felt like the ground had been pulled out from under me. The loss was immense, but his teachings and positivity remained a guiding light. I remember I was in a session far away from my home when my phone rang, and it was my sister on the call. I disconnected, but then she left a message which was a rare thing to do. I knew in my soul that just a few minutes earlier, a crystal glass left my hand and fell into pieces. A sign off on what was about to happen to my life in a while.

My phone had a notification, and I knew it was not a message I wanted to read. "He is no more" it read, as sent from my sister. I felt I lost my breath, but then I gathered myself as I had a long way to travel to reach my dad, who had already left for his heavenly abode.

After he left, I thought my world had ended. But then, just a day later, something incredible happened. I received my doctorate certificate, a milestone I had been working towards for years. Exactly a month later, I was awarded the Woman in Leadership in Human Resources by the Maldives Association of Human Resources.

I stood on stage, holding the award, and felt their presence. My parents weren't gone; they were with me, celebrating my achievements.

"Daddy, Mummy," I whispered under my breath, "Thank you."

Life has a way of showing you magic when you least expect it. Every time I've faced a situation that brought me to tears, something beautiful has followed. I believe it's my parents, working their magic from above. They're my angels, guiding me, my sister, and my brother.

"Do you miss them?" a friend asked me once.

"Every single day," I replied. "But they haven't gone anywhere. They're here, in every smile, every kind word, every hug."

Even now, as I write this, I feel their presence. Heena, who's helping me write this book, feels like a gift they sent. My job, the recognition I receive, and the wonderful people I meet—all of it feels like they're doing. It's as if their energy lives within me, guiding my steps and lighting my path.

"Daddy always said life is a circle," I told my brother one evening. "Do you think we've completed ours?"

He shook his head. "Not yet. But they did, and they've passed their energy on to us."

That energy, that love, is what keeps me going. I carry their words, their lessons, and their spirit in everything I do. They're not gone; they've simply moved to a place where they can watch over us more closely. And one day, when my circle is complete, I'll join them. Until then, I'll live with the power of three—my mother, father, and me.

AND he lives in
me happily ever
after

Write a letter to someone you lost in life.

BEHAVIORS MODELLED

Don't give examples. Be exemplary. Don't show the path, walk on it.

CHAPTER 3

Behaviours ...

I TAKE ACTION

As a child, I was always ready to take risks and embrace new challenges. I didn't just sit around thinking about what could be done; I took tangible actions to make things happen.

Whether it was climbing the guava tree in the neighbourhood, diving into the deepest part of the dense backyard, or walking alone in the evening, I was driven by a sense of curiosity and determination.

This proactive mindset allowed me to learn and grow from every experience, shaping me into someone who values action over hesitation and courage over comfort.

This proactive and risk-taking mindset from my childhood had a profound impact on my adulthood. Today, I take initiative, and the rest all fall into place.

My action-taking has turned me into a leader rather than just a boss. Whether it's in my career, personal projects, or relationships, I am likely the one who steps up to make things happen.

The driving force behind my TAKING ACTIONS is 'Faith,' the one I learnt from the verse,

"If you have faith the size of a mustard seed, you will say to this mountain, 'Move from here to there,' and it will move; and nothing will be impossible for you." (Matthew 17:20-21)

The phrase "if you have faith like a mustard seed" comes from a biblical parable and is often used to illustrate the power of even the smallest amount of faith. The mustard seed is one of the smallest, yet it grows into a large tree.

In practical terms, having faith like a mustard seed means believing in yourself and your abilities, even if that belief seems small or insignificant. It encourages you to take action and trust that your efforts, no matter how small, can lead to great results. This mindset can be incredibly empowering, helping you to overcome obstacles and achieve your goals.

To act from faith, one must take a single direction. You cannot function from a dual mindset. One must be direction- and decision-focused. It is not about right and wrong; it is about direction in the way of your faith.

Recollect one story of your life where you overcame a situation by taking action.

I BELIEVE IN PRAYERS

Prayers are wishes we make when we want one thing, and such prayers are answered because the desire is one, and the answer is one. I took the courage to believe that prayer is a powerful element in my life because my actions have a shield over them, just like the scratch guard on my phone protects it from cracking even if it falls. Similarly, my actions are guarded by prayers, ensuring they remain unbroken and resilient.

This belief in the power of prayer means that every step I take, and every decision I make, is enveloped in a layer of spiritual protection. Just as a scratch guard absorbs the impact and prevents damage to my phone, my prayers absorb the uncertainties and challenges of life, providing a buffer that keeps my actions intact and effective.

When I pray, or someone prays for me, I am not just wishing for an outcome; I am actively engaging in a process that aligns my desires with a higher purpose. This alignment brings clarity and focus, making my actions more deliberate and purposeful. The courage to believe in the power of prayer transforms my mindset, instilling confidence that my efforts are supported and safeguarded.

In moments of doubt or difficulty, this belief acts as a source of strength. Knowing that my actions are protected by prayers gives me the resilience to persevere, even when faced with obstacles. It reassures me that, just like the scratch guard on my phone, my prayers will prevent my efforts from shattering under pressure.

Ultimately, this faith in prayer as a protective shield empowers me to take risks and pursue my goals with a sense of security and peace. It is a reminder that I am not alone in my journey and that my actions are fortified by a powerful, unseen force that guides and protects me every step of the way.

I MOVE ON

Moving on is a second layer of action one should take. This is like putting both legs on the ground and walking in sync. As you walk with both feet hitting the ground with certainty, that's when the magic begins.

Elaborating on this idea, moving on involves not just taking the initial step, but continuing to move forward. It's about committing to the journey, much like walking requires both feet to work together in harmony. Each step you take builds momentum, propelling you forward and creating a rhythm that carries you through challenges and uncertainties.

When you move on with your feet firmly planted, you create a sense of balance and stability.

My feet represented my confidence and determination.

This grounded approach allows you to navigate obstacles with greater ease and resilience. Just as walking requires coordination and trust in your ability to maintain your stride, moving on requires faith in your capacity to handle whatever comes your way.

The magic begins when you embrace this process fully. As you walk with certainty, you start to see progress and growth. Each step reinforces your belief in your ability to move forward, and this confidence attracts new opportunities and possibilities. The journey itself becomes a source of strength and inspiration, revealing the potential within you to overcome challenges and achieve your goals.

Moving on is about taking continuous, deliberate actions with a sense of purpose and assurance. It's about trusting the process and believing in the power of forward momentum. When you do this, you unlock the magic of transformation and growth, turning each step into a meaningful part of your journey.

THOUGHTS MODELLED

Thoughts have the
power over 1440
minutes of your
day.

CHAPTER 4

Thoughts ...

DAILY THOUGHTS

Habits (actions) have a deeper root called thoughts.

Habits are routines or behaviours that we perform regularly, often without much conscious thought. They can be positive, like exercising daily, or negative, like biting our nails. Habits are formed through repetition and can become automatic over time.

Habits often stem from our underlying thoughts and beliefs. The way we think can significantly influence our actions and behaviours.

For example, if someone constantly thinks positively about their health, they're more likely to develop healthy habits like regular exercise and balanced eating.

Resonating ditto,

"Watch your thoughts, for they become words. Watch your words, for they become actions. Watch your actions, for they become habits. Watch your habits, for they become character. Watch your character, for it becomes

your destiny."
- Lao Tzu

Here are my FIVE daily thoughts; you might get inspired to make them yours, or how about you find your own?

- Practice Instinctive Decision
- Embrace Change
- Choose to Think Positive
- Celebrate Progress
- Remember my purpose

What are your TOP FIVE daily thoughts?

PRACTICE INSTINCTIVE DECISION

In times of making choices, we find ourselves navigating through layers of thoughts. The early thoughts often surface first because they are powerful and closely connected to our purpose, creating a strong connection. However, we know that we have the option to subside these thoughts by bringing in reasoning, calculations, and practicality. When we consciously assign our energies to all the thoughts that come to mind, those instinctive thoughts start to let go.

I strongly stand by these first thoughts that fought their way to the surface but often lost their battle against reasoning. I allow them to win daily by practicing instinctive decision-making. When I flushed those medicines away, picked up that crunchy guava, answered the first job call, or chose to be called by a new name, all these choices were made by instinct. I never regretted taking them; instead, I took ownership and marvelled at the outcomes.

One day, I was discussing this with my colleague, Sarah.

"I noticed you always seem so confident in your decisions. How do you do it?" asked Sarah.

"Sarah, I trust my instincts. When I make a choice, I go with my gut feeling first. It's usually the thought that surfaces first and feels the strongest," I responded. But what about reasoning and practicality? Don't you consider those?" asked Sarah.

I said, "I do, but I let my instincts lead. If my gut feeling aligns with my long-term vision, I follow it. Reasoning and practicality come into play, but they don't overshadow my initial instinct.". Sarah's eyes widened, and she asked, "That's interesting. Have you ever regretted a decision made by instinct?" "Not really. Even if things didn't go as planned, I take ownership of my choices and learn from them. It's about trusting yourself and your journey." I responded. As Steve Jobs once said,

"Have the courage to follow your heart and intuition. They somehow already know what you truly want to become."

Have you ever taken any decision instinctively?

EMBRACE CHANGE

Quoting the Greek philosopher Heraclitus,

"The only constant in life is change"

meaning that things are always changing, and nothing stays the same forever, is a favorite line used by one of my very close friend. He often uses it to respond to the question, "Hey! You have changed so much."

One day, I asked him, "Why do you always say that?"

He smiled and replied, "Because it's true. Change is the only constant in life. Embracing it makes us stronger and more adaptable."

I nodded, reflecting on his words. "I agree. Change is inevitable and a constant part of all processes. Embracing this change and carrying a mindset to accept it instead of challenging it is a deliberate action one must take.

Do not fight change.

“Accept Change “is my daily thought that I remind myself of and practice whenever I need to.

My transition from Choti to Dr. Annepaul Vemagiri happened organically as each name added a character I played, and I played it well.

My shift from a teacher to Heading the Learning & Development Operations had many positions where I didn’t want to let go. I wanted to hold on to my old self, but when I finally did let go, the new one became my favourite spot. Moving from one profession to another, I realized they were all beads of the same string which is my passion. I could allow the lace to form only when I accepted the change and moved to the next career. Instead of staying in my comfort zone, I allowed myself to move and move and move.

When I travelled for work from India to Doha, to UAE, to Bahrain, and now to the Maldives, I accepted the change of culture and embraced it to become a part of my new being. Along the way, I met many people and carried all their warmth and energies that took me this far. Today, I am happy I travelled.

As Winston Churchill once said,

“To improve is to change; to be perfect is to change often.”

This quote resonates deeply with my journey and the lessons I’ve learnt along the way.

How do you see change in life?

CHOOSE TO THINK POSITIVE

The art of choosing the positive has been ingrained in me because I am a chip off the old block that is my dad. I learnt this art of finding a positive outlook in every situation in life.

One night in Chennai, my car broke down in the middle of the night. It was a stressful and frustrating experience. Stranded on a dark, deserted road, I felt a wave of panic. Thankfully, I managed to get home safely, but the car was in bad shape.

The next morning, I called Dad to tell him what had happened.

"Dad, my car broke down last night. I was so scared and stressed out," I said.

Without missing a beat, he reassured me, "Don't worry, we'll get this sorted out."

True to his word, Dad sprang into action. He contacted the insurance company, filed the necessary claims, and arranged for the car to be towed to a reputable repair shop.

Within three days, the car was back in perfect working order. Dad had handled everything with his usual efficiency and calm demeanour. When he handed me the keys, he said with a smile, "See? No need to stress. It's all taken care of, and from now onwards you will be excellent in driving the car as the worst is over."

"How do you always manage to stay so positive, Dad?" I asked, still in awe.

He chuckled and replied, "It's all about perspective. Every challenge is an opportunity to learn and grow. Remember that, and you'll be just fine."

How he could see a positive perspective even in a situation like this has been an awe-inspiring moment for me to this day. Dad's ability to turn a stressful situation into a manageable one was just another example of why he was always my go-to person in times of trouble. I learnt many such lessons from my dad and made it my daily thought process.

Choosing positivity daily means making a conscious decision each morning to focus on the good in my life and approach each situation with an optimistic mindset. This involves being mindful of my thoughts and emotions, practicing gratitude, and using positive affirmations to set a hopeful tone for the day. Engaging in acts of kindness, maintaining healthy habits, and building resilience in the face of challenges are also key components. Surrounding myself with positive influences and limiting exposure to negativity further supports this mindset. By consistently choosing positivity, I can enhance my well-being and create a more joyful and fulfilling life.

As Dad always said,

"Life is 10% what happens to us and 90% how we react to it."

What do you choose daily?
POSITIVE or?

CELEBRATE PROGRESS

Embracing progress daily means actively seeking and welcoming growth and improvement in various aspects of your life. It involves setting achievable goals, taking consistent actions towards them, and learning from both successes and setbacks. By maintaining a positive attitude and viewing challenges as opportunities for growth, you cultivate a mindset of continuous improvement and resilience. Celebrating even small milestones along the way helps to reinforce your commitment to progress. This approach can lead to significant personal and professional development over time, fostering a sense of fulfillment and achievement.

Every morning, I wake up with a sense of purpose. Instead of creating a daily to-do list, I embrace a different philosophy:

So instead of a TO DO list, I follow a simple rule. I DO the list.

My long-term vision is my guiding star, and every task I complete today is a step towards that bigger goal.

As the day begins, I prioritize my tasks based on their alignment with my vision. I tackle the most crucial ones first, ensuring that my energy is directed towards what truly matters. When unexpected tasks arise, I assess their importance and urgency. If they contribute to my long-term goals, I integrate them into my workflow. If not, I handle them efficiently, ensuring they don't derail my focus.

This approach keeps me motivated and productive. Each completed task is a small victory, bringing me closer to my dreams. By the end of the day, I feel accomplished, knowing that I've made meaningful progress. This is my story, and every day, I write a new chapter.

As the famous quote by Lao Tzu goes,

"The journey of a thousand miles begins with one step."

Each task I complete today is one step closer to my ultimate vision.

What is your progress graph?
DAILY or YEARLY?

REMEMBER MY PURPOSE

I believe purpose is the core. When my purpose is unclear, no matter how well I plan my path, getting lost is definite. When my purpose is clear, it acts like a beacon, guiding me through various paths and ensuring I stay on course, even if the journey takes unexpected turns. Conversely, without a clear purpose, even the most meticulously planned paths can lead to confusion and a sense of being lost.

It's a reminder that understanding my "why" can make all the difference in how I navigate my life. If I understand my why daily, every task becomes meaningful, and the quality of my day improves. If I am still in search of my purpose and haven't got the clarity, which is usually the case before one day I know it, then I replace purpose with happiness. It means what makes me happy and content. I do what brings joy to my soul. I find one thing in my daily tasks that brings happiness. It could be as simple as dancing in the rain or buying myself an ice cream.

I usually love watching movies as a habit every day. It gives me happiness and makes me get lost in a world that's not mine. I also love drinking water, a small act to feel refreshed when I'm worked up. At times, taking a walk with my ears listening to the same favourite song. All this connects me to my greater purpose, which is to train. Movies help me find stories to tell during my training, drinking water keeps my mind flushed, and taking a walk gives me the right energy to hold long sessions. When I do things that bring me happiness, then the same finds its way to my purpose.

"Hey, I love how you've found ways to integrate happiness into your daily routine. It's inspiring!" asked my friend.

"Yes, I do. I love watching movies that have strong storytelling elements. They give me great material for my training sessions. As for songs, I have a few favourites that I listen to on repeat during my walks. They really help me clear my mind and stay energized."

It makes a huge difference. Even small acts like drinking water or taking a short walk can refresh our minds and keep us connected to our purpose.

I love this quote on purpose,

"Your purpose in life is to find your purpose and give your whole heart and soul to it." Buddha

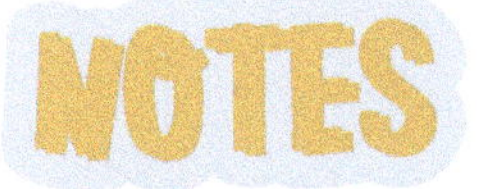

How do you address your daily purpose?

MY LEARNINGS WHILE WRITING THIS BOOK

Learning always
leaves its footprints

CHAPTER 5

Learnings ...

HALF WINGED BUTTERFLY

My life story is that of a half-winged butterfly. Despite facing arthritis, divorce, and the loss of my parents, my determination to overcome is a testament to an enduring human spirit.

As Maya Angelou said,

"We may encounter many defeats, but we must not be defeated."

This quote resonates deeply with my journey, reminding me that while I have faced significant challenges, I continue to rise and inspire others with my unwavering spirit.

When I spoke to my sister, I said, "Sometimes I feel like a half-winged butterfly." My sister asked what I meant, and I explained that it symbolizes a state of transition and incomplete transformation. Despite facing challenges, I feel like I'm still growing. Usha agreed, saying those were the wings I lost, but I still have the wing of overcoming every situation with a mindset to win. She added that my journey inspires her and others. I thanked her, expressing my desire to help others see that even with challenges, we can still fly.

Later, I shared the same metaphor with my coach. He found it interesting and asked what it meant to me. I explained my growth despite challenges. He acknowledged my strength and resilience, asking how I plan to continue. I said, I want to inspire others and take them under my half wing, showing them that we can achieve great things despite challenges. My coach applauded my goal, encouraging me to keep pushing forward.

What is your half-winged story?

MY LEARNING WHILE WRITING THIS BOOK

My journey with Heena has been incredibly profound and transformative. Since 2022, she has been coaching me to write, and I feel a deep, almost mystical connection with her, as if, we are linked by an invisible thread from a past life. We've had our ups and downs, moments where we agreed to disagree, and times when we let go of each other, only to find ourselves working together on my second book.

When we started writing my second book, I decided to surrender instead of trying to control the process. This decision was a turning point for me. The moment I chose to surrender, I realized that I had been in control all along. I began to say yes to everything Heena suggested, and the process became like a mesmerizing dance where we both flowed together. It felt like I was in a dream, moving in the direction of my purpose. Heena and I connected on a deeper level, feeling each other's emotions and growing stronger together.

This experience taught me that in any relationship, whether with a parent, colleague, friend, or lover, it's important to let go. Letting go means surrendering, loosening, and flowing.

Reflecting on this, I remembered a childhood memory. I was about six years old.

I was sitting on the side berth of a train while we were travelling on a train during summer vacation. The train had halted, and my parents stepped down at the station to get me a surprise. They brought me an ice cream cone, something magical to my six-year-old eyes. My dad handed it to me, signalling me to hold it with both hands.

"Wow, it looks so pretty! What is it?" I screamed. "It's an ice cream cone. Just hold it gently; don't squeeze it too hard," alerted my dad. "Okay, I'll try," I said, but in vain. "Oops, it's melting! I'm sorry, Daddy."

Nervous and excited, I gripped it tightly, but the ice cream started melting and dripping down my frock.

I saw the disappointment in my parents' eyes and felt ashamed for ruining their joy. This memory resurfaced while I was learning to surrender. I realized that holding on too tightly can cause us to lose what we cherish. To enjoy something delicate, like a relationship, I must hold it with care, not with a grip that melts away its essence, but with gentleness and calm.

This realization has deeply impacted my writing and my relationship with Heena. It has taught me to embrace the journey with an open heart and to cherish the delicate balance of surrender and control.

To enjoy something delicate like a relationship, I must hold it with care. Not with a grip to melt away the essence of the relationship but surrendering to its softness, being extremely gentle and calm.

Surrender means letting go of the need to control and allowing things to unfold naturally. It's about trusting the process and being open to whatever comes our way, without trying to force or manipulate outcomes. In relationships, surrendering means being gentle and accepting, allowing the connection to flow and grow organically.

In my journey with Heena, surrendering has allowed me to experience a deeper, more harmonious collaboration. By letting go of control, I've been able to connect more deeply and create something beautiful together This is my second book.

My AirPods nowadays play a song for sure on a loop.

I surrender all

I surrender all

All to Thee my blessed Savior

I surrender all

What has been your learning reading "from END to AND"?

IF YOU WANT TO CONTROL LET GO ...

This book, "From END to AND," was written and published in 10 days. When Heena and I came together during our first meeting. We were excited and wanted this book to be special. So we thought, why not make it a ready-to-book version of that instant publishing? Our strategy has been simple

We first surrendered to the idea

We then let go of the control

We used 4 eyes and 10 fingers to add to the speed ;)

I was writing every day and at any time of the day, flowing with the flow of thoughts

What you read is the work of two geniuses who let go to take control of their handiwork.

Thank you Heena, for the Tango.

About the Author

My experience spans over 26 years, with 12 years dedicated to teaching hospitality academics and 14 years to training hotel operations. My expertise in learning and development is exceptional.

I earned my doctorate in learning & development from the Asian College of Teachers in collaboration with European International University (EIU-Paris). My research led to the renowned Train The Trainer Program, now a core part of the Brand–Atmosphere, where I oversee Learning & Development for nine iconic island resorts and support projects in India.

My career includes working with hospitality brands in India, Qatar, UAE, and Bahrain. As a philanthropist and co-author of the book "Knock! Knock! Who's there? CULTURE," available on Amazon and Flipkart, I am also an ICF-Certified professional coach.

My achievements include numerous accolades, such as the Excellence WOMEN in HR Award by MAHRP 2023, the Academic Excellence Award 2023 by Asian Education Conclave, and the Corporate Trainer Award 2023 by the Asian College of Teachers.

You can connect with me on:

- https://www.linkedin.com/in/drannepaulvemagiri
- https://www.instagram.com/knockknockwriters
- https://amzn.in/d/1QYKNAW

Also by Dr. Annepaul Vemagiri

Amazon Link

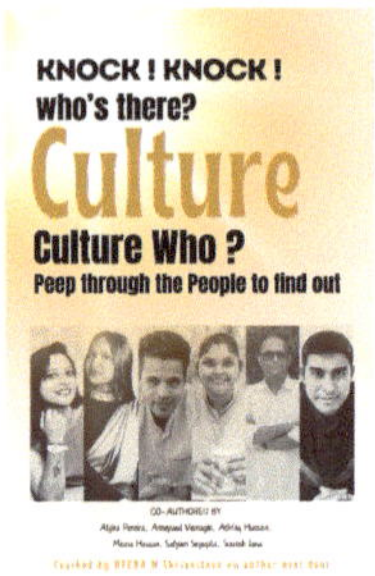

Knock Knock! Who's there? It's Culture!Culture Who? Peep Through the People to Find Out
The book is a perfect mix to write about culture and development.

Do you really understand culture and development?

The same question was asked to these six writers, and their answers became a book filled with insightful perspectives that will resonate with everyone.

Dive into a rich tapestry of ideas and experiences that challenge and enlighten, offering a unique lens on how culture shapes development and vice versa.

This book is a must-read for anyone looking to deepen their understanding of these intertwined concepts.

www.ingramcontent.com/pod-product-compliance
Lightning Source LLC
LaVergne TN
LVHW021251160826
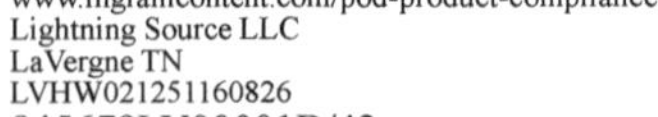
845679LV00001B/43

* 9 7 9 8 8 9 7 2 4 1 6 1 3 *